www.FlowerpotPress.com
PAB-0808-0342 · 978-1-4867-2639-4
Made in China/Fabriqué en Chine

Copyright © 2023 Flowerpot Press,
a Division of Flowerpot Children's Press, Inc., Oakville, ON, Canada, and Kamalu LLC,
Franklin, TN, U.S.A. All rights reserved. Can you find the flowerpot? No part of this
publication may be reproduced, stored in a retrieval system or transmitted, in any
form or by any means, electronic, mechanical, photocopying, recording, optical scan,
or otherwise, without the prior written permission of the copyright holder.

Finn's Fun Trucks
MILITARY MACHINES

Written by Finn Coyle Illustrated by Srimalie Bassani

We are members of the U.S. military. We do our jobs with the help of military machines.

Each machine is used in a different branch of the military. Can you guess what each machine is?

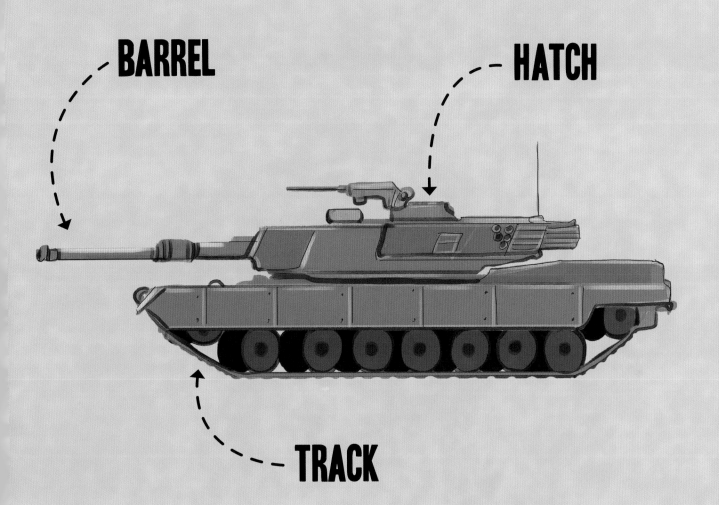

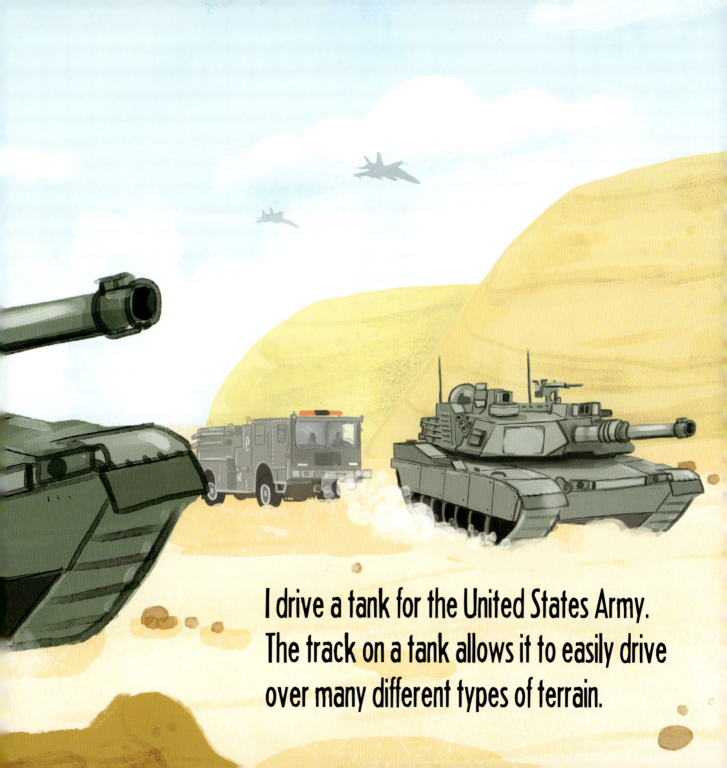

I drive a tank for the United States Army. The track on a tank allows it to easily drive over many different types of terrain.

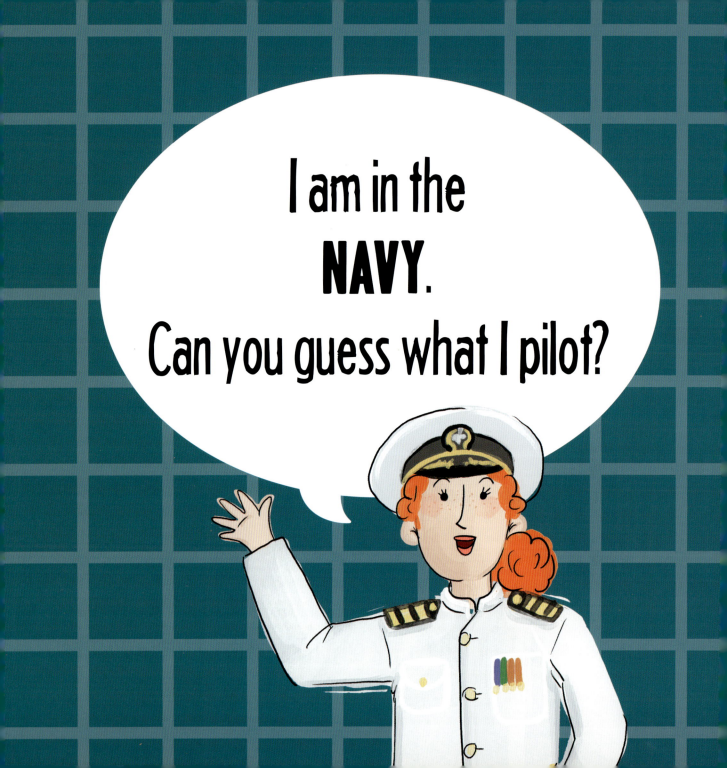

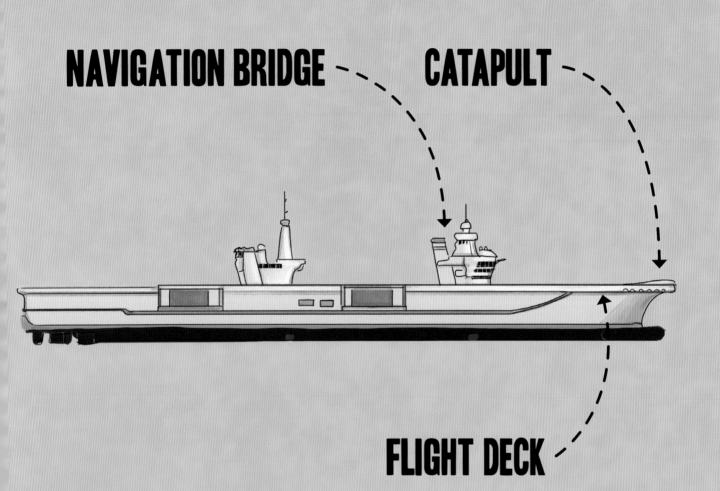

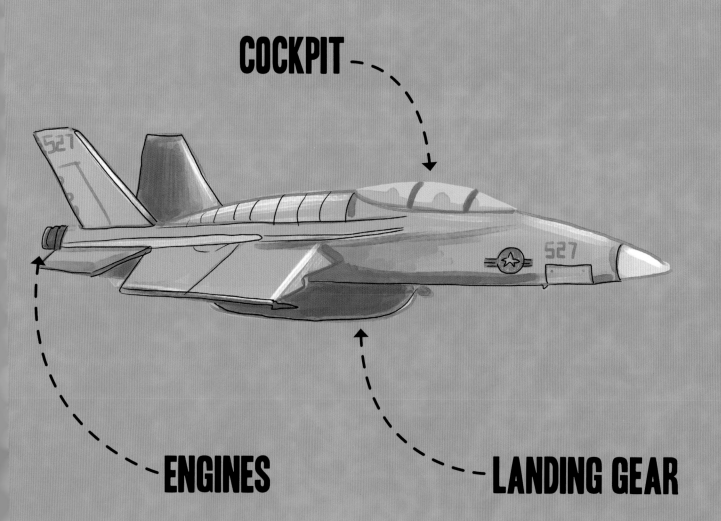

I fly a fighter jet for the United States Air Force. The powerful engines on the jet allow it to fly at speeds up to thousands of miles per hour.

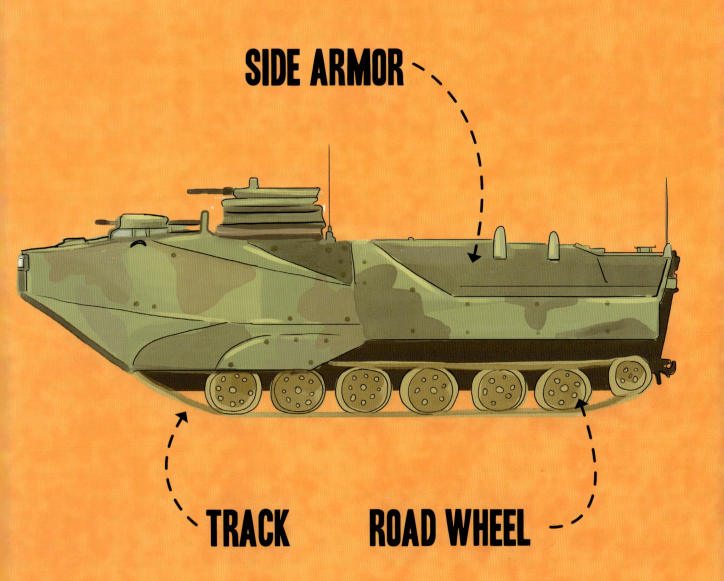

I drive an amphibious assault vehicle for the United States Marines. This machine can carry troops from ships onto the shore.

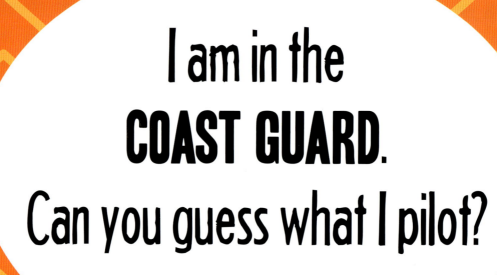

I am in the **COAST GUARD.**
Can you guess what I pilot?

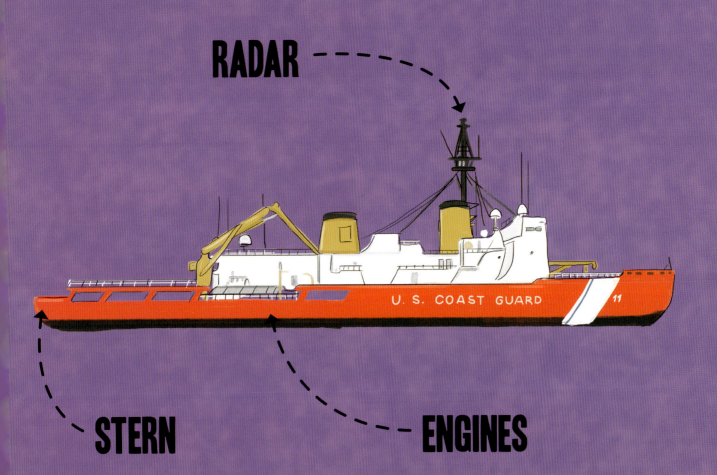

I pilot a Coast Guard cutter for the United States Coast Guard. These ships can be used to break through icy seas, perform search and rescues, and enforce laws.

We are the United States Armed Forces. Can you guess what we can do when we all work together?

We can protect our fellow citizens!

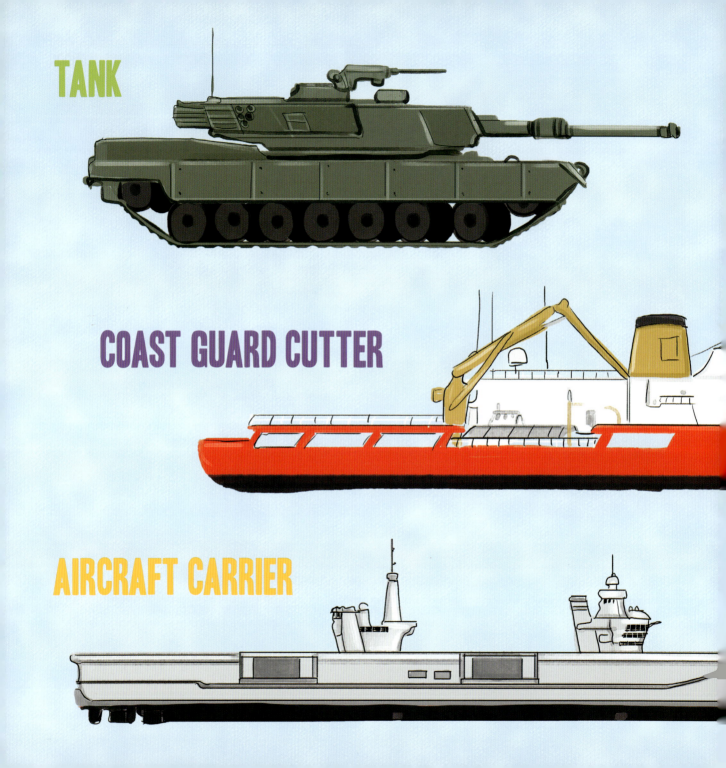

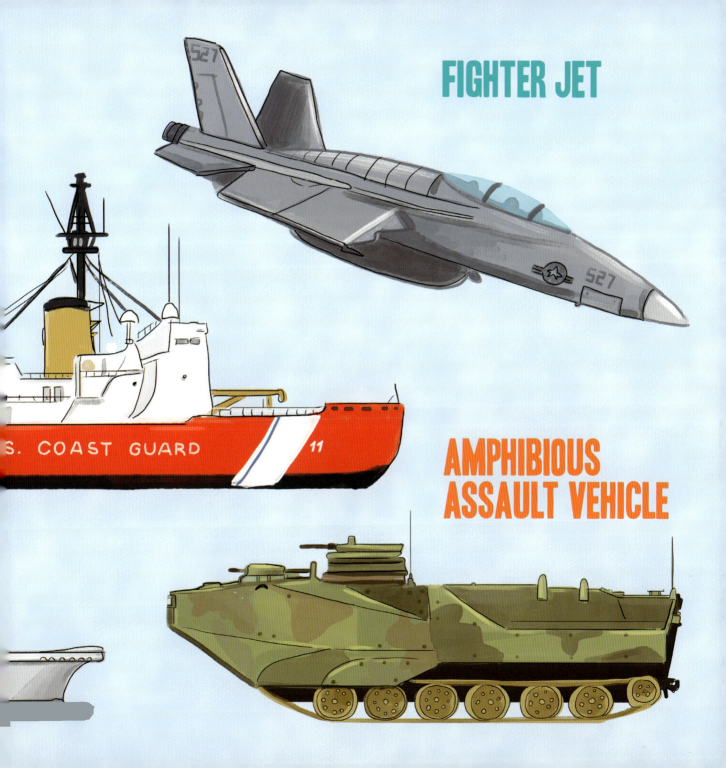